What Do I Look Like?

Anders Hanson

Consulting Editor, Diane Craig, M.A./Reading Specialist

ABDO Publishing Company

Published by ABDO Publishing Company, 4940 Viking Drive, Edina, Minnesota 55435.

Printed in the United States.

Credits
Edited by: Pam Price
Curriculum Coordinator: Nancy Tuminelly
Cover and Interior Design and Production: Mighty Media
Photo Credits: AbleStock, Brand X Pictures, Photodisc, Stockbyte, Wewerka Photography

Library of Congress Cataloging-in-Publication Data

Hanson, Anders, 1980-
      What do I look like? / Anders Hanson.
          p. cm. -- (First words)
      Includes index.
      ISBN 1-59679-442-9 (hardcover)
      ISBN 1-59679-443-7 (paperback)
          1. Vocabulary--Juvenile literature. I. Title. II. First words (ABDO Publishing Company)
      PE1449.H2469 2005
      428.1--dc22
                                                                                              2005041243

SandCastle™ books are created by a professional team of educators, reading specialists, and content developers around five essential components that include phonemic awareness, phonics, vocabulary, text comprehension, and fluency. All books are written, reviewed, and leveled for guided reading, early intervention reading, and Accelerated Reader® programs and designed for use in shared, guided, and independent reading and writing activities to support a balanced approach to literacy instruction.

Let Us Know

After reading the book, SandCastle would like you to tell us your stories about reading. What is your favorite page? Was there something hard that you needed help with? Share the ups and downs of learning to read. We want to hear from you! To get posted on the ABDO Publishing Company Web site, send us e-mail at:

sandcastle@abdopub.com

SandCastle Level: Beginning

About This Series

The *First Words* series provides emerging readers with multiple opportunities to practice reading high-frequency words used in simple text. These books are appropriate for independent, shared, and guided reading.

Red Rebus Section (pages 4–11) Each spread features a predictable, repetitive rebus sentence with a familiar picture clue placed opposite a full-page photograph that strongly supports the text.

Blue Story Section (pages 12–17) An illustrated short story containing the featured sight words offers contextual, repetitive reading opportunities using simple text and familiar letter-sound correspondence.

Green Game Section (pages 18–21) A fun, read-together guessing game based upon the contents of the book expands vocabulary and increases comprehension.

Rebus Glossary (page 22) This list pairs the words and picture clues featured in the rebus sentences.

SandCastle First Thirty Sight Words List (page 23) Use this list to build phonics and word recognition strategies for emerging and beginning readers.

Sight Word Focus

| a | I | like | look |

I look like a  .

I look like a  .

I look like an  .

I look like a .

What Do I Look Like?

Abby looks like
a princess.

Jason looks like
a pirate.

What do I look like?

Look at me!

My dad is a king.

I wear dresses.

I have a crown.

What am I?

I am a princess!

Rebus Glossary

angel

pirate

princess

witch

SandCastle
First Thirty Sight Words

a	here	not
am	I	on
and	in	said
are	is	see
at	it	the
big	like	this
can	little	to
come	look	up
for	me	we
go	my	you

About SandCastle™

A professional team of educators, reading specialists, and content developers created the SandCastle™ series to support young readers as they develop reading skills and strategies and increase their general knowledge. The SandCastle™ series has four levels that correspond to early literacy development in young children. The levels are provided to help teachers and parents select the appropriate books for young readers.

Emerging Readers
(no flags)

Beginning Readers
(1 flag)

Transitional Readers
(2 flags)

Fluent Readers
(3 flags)

These levels are meant only as a guide. All levels are subject to change.

To see a complete list of SandCastle™ books and other nonfiction titles from ABDO Publishing Company, visit www.abdopub.com or contact us at:

4940 Viking Drive, Edina, Minnesota 55435 • 1-800-800-1312 • fax: 1-952-831-1632